ESSENTIAL

INVESTING IN HIGH TECH

MICHAEL MURPHY, CFA
AND
MARC ROBINSON

DORLING KINDERSLEY

London • New York • Sydney • Delhi • Paris • Munich • Johannesburg

A DORLING KINDERSLEY BOOK

Editor Stephanie Rubenstein
Design and Layout Jill Dupont
Photography Anthony Nex
Project Editor Crystal A. Coble
Senior Art Editor Mandy Earey
Photo Research Mark Dennis, Sam Ruston
Indexing Rachel Rice
Editorial Director LaVonne Carlson
Design Director Tina Vaughan
Publisher Sean Moore

First American Edition, 2000
24681097531
Published in the United States by
Dorling Kindersley Publishing, Inc.
95 Madison Avenue,
New York, New York 10016

Packaged by Top Down Productions

CONTENTS

THE
INDUSTRIES

COLLECTING
INFORMATION

INTRODUCTION

From time to time, economies go through rapid changes creating massive new opportunities while old structures are destroyed. We're now living through one of those major changes, and it's possible to envision some rare opportunities to build new wealth. There's no doubt we're in a new technology economy. Our infrastructure is changing from highways, airports, and radio/TV broadcasting to satellites, fiber optics, and wireless connectivity. Investing in High Tech can help you make sense of the new technologies, consumer demands, cost structures, and educational needs of the new economy. It can also help you take steps toward participating successfully in this historic economic and social transformation that's providing extraordinary investment opportunities.

GETTING STARTED

In 1982, *Time* magazine named the computer
as its "Man of the Year." By then—if not earlier—high
technology had ushered in the dawn of a new economy.

THE NEW ECONOMY

What actually is the new economy? Are we truly in a revolutionary stage as significant as the industrial revolution was in the late 1800s?

WHAT'S HIGH TECHNOLOGY?

High technology is a group of industries within our economy. It's made up of companies that use research and development (R&D) combined with advanced thinking to produce new products. The term is often thought to be synonymous with electronics, but also includes the latest advances in chemistry and biology, particularly in healthcare. Because it's central to high technology, R&D spending may be the key to identifying high tech investment opportunities.

A very complex product may not necessarily be high tech. For example, the car is no longer considered a high tech product, although it was when it was invented.

WHAT'S A HIGH TECH STOCK?

A high tech stock is a share of ownership in a company that produces rapidly advancing designs as a result of heavy investments in R&D.

PACKING THEM IN ▶
Here's just one example of how dramatically a computer chip has advanced. In 1978, an Intel 8086 could hold 29,000 transistors. By 1995, an Intel Pentium Pro could carry 5.5 million transistors. In 2000, the Intel Pentium III chip could support 9.5 million transistors.

GRASPING THE CONCEPT OF PROGRESS

If, over the past 30 years, the size, cost, performance, and energy efficiency of transportation technology had improved at the same rate as information technology, a car would:
- Be as small as a toaster;
- Go 100,000 miles an hour;
- Get 150,000 miles to the gallon;
- Cost a mere $200.

But, as auto executives like to point out, your car might often stop working while speeding down the road, forcing you to find a safe way to stop. Then you'd have to turn off the car and turn it on again to clear the problem.

MILESTONES IN HIGH TECHNOLOGY

Here are some watershed events in the development of the high tech industry:

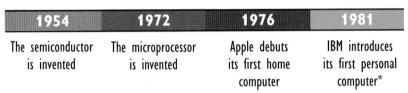

1954	1972	1976	1981
The semiconductor is invented	The microprocessor is invented	Apple debuts its first home computer	IBM introduces its first personal computer*

* Computers began changing from a U.S. corporate business to a worldwide consumer business.

▶ **A FIRST**
This is a replica of the first transistor ever made. It was developed by Bell Labs (the research wing of AT&T) in 1948.

HIGH TECH'S ROLE IN THE ECONOMY

The new economy is bringing with it changes in how people work and how they view and manage their resources. We're becoming less dependent on cars and roads and more dependent on computers, phones, and information networks to live out our daily lives.

WILL IT LAST?

It's impossible to predict the future with absolute certainty, but simply consider the cell phone to see how much a new advance can change our thinking.

For example, not long ago people thought that if there were a million cell phones we would use up all the available radio spectrum. Now we know you can have one billion cell phones and still have room for another billion. There will be approximately 435 million cell phones sold worldwide in 2000 and projections are for a billion within a few years.

Original cell phones were *analog* so they needed a large amount of *bandwidth* to capture the variations in our voices.

IT'S A QUOTE

"We're a society moving electronic bits instead of molecules." - Nicholas Negreponte, MIT Media Lab Director

Today, with the move into digital technology, voices can be packaged in compact ways and sent through channels much more efficiently. Thousands of conversations can now be packed into the space once required for a single call. This kind of efficiency is being experienced by every high tech industry. We're just beginning to feel the power of high tech's potential.

IN FIVE YEARS...

Today, 7.4% of the world's population have cell phones. In five years, that number is projected to be over 21%.

Only 3.3% of the world's population has Internet access. In five years, it's projected to almost triple to about 9.6%.

Only 1.7% of the world's population owns a computer. In five years, that number is projected to more than double to 4%.

Only about one-third of the world's population has ever made a phone call. What will that number be in five years?

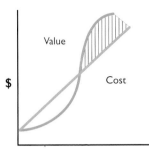

Number of Users

◀ METCALFE'S LAW

The chart on the left illustrates a phenomenon known as Metcalfe's Law (after Robert Metcalfe, founder of 3Com). It explains that the more people use a network, the more valuable it becomes. For example, if two people are connected by computer, they can only communicate back and forth. But each time a new person is connected, the connectivity increases exponentially (10 users make 100 connections, 20 users make 400 connections, because everyone becomes connected to everyone else). Once the network reaches critical mass, the value of the network becomes greater than its cost, and the network becomes almost irresistible to the remaining people who are not yet users.

▼ FIBER OPTICS

Transmitting information—including voice and imagery—is rapidly evolving. Huge transcontinental cables of copper wiring are being replaced by bundles of ultra-thin fiber optic threads that are lowering costs and dramatically increasing speed and connectivity. Each white light is divided into many different colors and each color can carry data.

WHAT DOES THE FUTURE HOLD?

Here are some reasonable forecasts for the near future:

- Videoconferencing systems will soon take the place of a lot of business air travel.
- Voice input will control your computer, most of your appliances and many of the workings in your car.
- Coming soon are solid state tape recorders with no moving parts.
- Within five years all long distance calls will be free.
- Video telephones will spread rapidly into homes. Cellular video phones will follow.
- Within 5 to 10 years there will be workable therapies for many solid tumor cancers. Many more diseases will be preventable and others will be curable.

WHY INVEST IN HIGH TECH?

Despite all of the dramatic growth and change in our economy and lifestyle, one can expect a lot more to come. An entirely new infrastructure is still emerging, so investors still have plenty of time.

WHERE GROWTH IS

Technology is becoming the largest—and is already the fastest—growing sector or our entire economy. Some key areas of technology growth are:

- Technology exports;
- Communications;
- Electronics;
- Medical;
- Biotechnology;
- Entertainment.

> **I** Technology companies tend to sell their products worldwide, so growth can continue despite slowdowns in one area of the world.

A REVOLUTION FOR ALL TIME

Many years of growth still lie ahead for investors. The world is in the midst of probably the greatest transformation it has ever experienced—if for no other reason than for the first time, the entire globe is participating. In almost unimaginable leaps and bounds, many aspects of our lives, from food and shelter to health and leisure, are being analyzed and restructured. Most of all, the technology revolution is changing the way we think and possibly the way we feel.

The earlier you make a decision to allocate some investment assets to the technology sector, the better your potential for high returns may be.

Shifting Sectors of the US Economy

This chart shows how our economy is expected to shift from nontechnology to technology industries over the next 7 years.

Year	Technology	Nontechnology
1997	15.0%	85.0%
1998	17.2	82.8
1999	19.6	80.4
2000	22.3	77.7
2001	25.3	74.4
2002	28.5	71.5
2003	31.9	68.1
2004	35.5	64.5
2005	39.3	60.7
2006	43.2	56.8
2007	47.3	52.7
2008	51.3	48.7

CTSL 30 Technologies

▲ **THE RISE IN PRICES**
This chart, representing the stocks in the California Technology Stock Letter Index, shows the rise in those stock prices over the past few years.

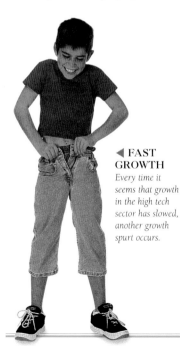

◀ **FAST GROWTH**
Every time it seems that growth in the high tech sector has slowed, another growth spurt occurs.

THE PHENOMENON OF EXPONENTIAL PROGRESS

In 1965, Gordon Moore (co-founder of Intel) predicted that the transistor density of semiconductor chips would double roughly every 18 months. This means that every year or two, the amount of computer processing speed you could buy for a dollar would double. This statement has come to be known as Moore's Law, and many experts expect it to continue to hold true for at least the next ten years.

At some point, the physical capacity of silicon, the material used to make most chips, may be reached, causing the entire technology to be redesigned. On the other hand, we may discover a new material that will enable electronics technology to continue developing at the same, or even faster rates. Even now, for example, scientists and engineers are looking at the potential of DNA to take over the role of silicon in transmitting electrical information.

11

HIGH TECH: HOW IT WORKS

In order to understand investment opportunities in high tech stocks, you first have to have some understanding of the world they live in.

IT STARTS WITH RESEARCH

Innovation comes from researching new ideas.
There are two kinds of research to understand.

BASIC RESEARCH

This kind of research is conducted in order to understand a basic scientific process: how something works. It's not aimed at a product but at a phenomenon. Sequencing the human genome is a good example. Scientists have cracked the DNA code (see pg. 13) which gives others opportunities to apply that broad knowledge to create new products. Another example is the discovery that a laser's white light can be split into colors and that each color can individually carry data in digital form through a fiber optics line. That has changed the face of communications.

APPLIED RESEARCH

Once a new principle is proven through basic research—that something in biology, physics, or chemistry works—scientists are able to say with certainty that a particular event will occur. At that point, scientists and engineers can begin to apply that knowledge to building a new, or improving on an existing product. That's called applied research (applying basic research solutions to a specific product problem). Trying to build a product before knowing whether it will work almost always fails. First you have to prove the underlying scientific principles to know that it will work.

THE HUMAN GENOME

A genome is one piece of DNA stretched out full-length. It's made up of every gene in your body plus other material that affects the gene. There are three main components of the genome project:

Mapping. This shows where every part of the genome is in relation to each other;

Sequencing. This identifies each individual gene and where it's located;

Annotating. This means learning and labeling the function of every component in the genome.

Sequencing the human genome has transformed biology to the point where scientists can now literally create the DNA they're looking for and focus on specific genetic targets.

For example, they can track the way a disease begins, which parts of the genome are turned on and off, and which genes are fighting back.

Genomics-based biology may pay off enormously in new drugs and diagnostic products. It may also let us map where a tumor is, identify it very precisely, and use guided surgery, where a computer guides the surgeon, to remove the tumor.

In a nutshell, every gene becomes a potential target for developing treatments and cures.

Other genomes. Scientists are already deeply involved in mapping the genomes of other things, such as viruses, bacteria, and yeast.

MICROTUNEOLOGY

The science of nanotechnology has produced a guitar no bigger than a blood cell. The guitar, 10 micrometers long, has six strummable strings.

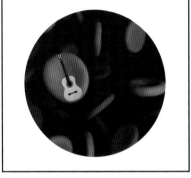

▼ THE POWER OF CHEMISTRY

Not long ago, the rule of thumb in chemistry R&D was that one scientist working one week could produce one new molecule. Today, one scientist, in a single day, can produce 100,000 new molecules. Try to imagine what the rate will be when this girl grows up.

PATENTS

The race for scientific breakthroughs often becomes a race for legal property ownership claims based upon the discovery.

PATENTS

Patents, the securing of exclusive rights to a specific design, are an important factor in the success of high tech companies. By recruiting top creative minds for their research teams, providing competitive salaries and benefits, and offering wide latitude for exploring new ideas, companies compete to secure a lead position in their field.

Recruiting requires a mix of talent who will focus on different aspects of developing successful products, and who can work well together. A company hopes to encourage the development of ideas that can become patented in the company's name and secure a proprietary advantage for them. They do this by creating a team environment, a creative atmosphere, and fostering a sense of commitment to an overall vision and goal.

PROPRIETARY ADVANTAGE

By patenting its home-grown ideas, a company acquires certain rights to a unique design that prevents others from copying the idea outright. Copying is something that could be accomplished easily by a competitor who could simply buy the product, take it apart, then build its own version using what was learned in the process of taking it apart.

A patent entitles its holder to sue any competitors who employ "substantially similar" designs for their own product after the patent has been filed. A competitor, therefore, must either negotiate the right to use the patent or come up with a design that's substantially different but accomplishes the same thing. That choice is typically made based on which route would be less expensive and less time consuming, or whether the competitor believes it can create a better design than the one that earned the patent.

NO MORE INVENTIONS

In 1875, the director of the U.S. Patent Office sent his resignation and advised that his department be closed. There was nothing left to invent, he claimed.

HIGH TECH?

As of 1940, a total of 90 patents in the U.S. had been taken out on shaving mugs.

GREEK LAWNS

A device invented as a primitive steam engine by the Greek engineer Hero, about the time of the birth of Christ, is used today as a rotating lawn sprinkler.

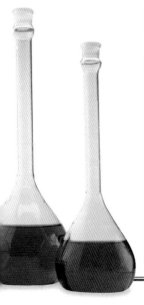

THREE WAYS TO USE PATENTS

Companies can use their patents in a variety of ways.

For cash. A patent doesn't have to be for the purpose of blocking competition. A company can license its patent rather than make the item itself. Texas Instruments (TI), for example, is still receiving over $100 million in royalties a year after licensing its basic semiconductor patents many years ago and regularly updating them. Anyone who makes a semiconductor pays TI.

For access. A company can do something called *cross licensing*. This means it can use patents for barter. Basically, it's a system of "I will give you access to my patent if you give me access to yours." IBM has possibly the largest patent library, spanning so many areas that they often barter their own patents for royalty-free patents to the latest high tech advances.

To create a company. A business can form a company that does nothing but license its patents. These *intellectual property* (IP) companies don't actually make anything. All they do is invent things, then license their patent rights to other companies who want to make the patented product.

WHO'S WORTH WHAT AND HOW

Of the seven richest people in America (based on the Forbes magazine survey for 2000), six made their fortunes in high tech. Take a look:

Who?	What?	How?
Bill Gates	63 billion	Microsoft
Larry Ellison	58 billion	Oracle
Paul Allen	36 billion	Microsoft
Warren Buffett	28 billion	Stock market
Gordon Moore	26 billion	Intel
Philip Anschutz	18 billion	Qwest
Steven Ballmer	17 billion	Microsoft

HOW HIGH TECH COMPANIES WORK

High tech companies are in the business of creating products no one knows they want—let alone one day need—since the product has never existed, or hasn't existed in the form being created. The long-term success of a company depends on a continuous cycle of R&D and sales.

❶ CREATE A PRODUCT

By their very nature, high tech companies are typically on the leading edge of a market—the frontier of the economy. They're delving into the unknown in order to bring something into the realm of the known and sell it in a market that doesn't yet exist. There are, however, advantages and disadvantages to being a pioneer.
Advantage. If the product turns out to be valuable, there will be no competition, at least until some other company catches on and starts to develop their own similar version of that product. Meanwhile, the advantage of being first enables a company to charge a premium for it, because it's a new or better product.
Disadvantages. There's considerable risk that what's being explored won't result in a successful product, or if there is a product, it won't be as valuable as one would hope.

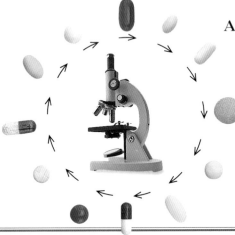

A CONTINUOUS CYCLE

The mark of a well-managed high tech company is the continuous cycle of investment in R&D and the ability to promote marketable products effectively, resulting in high growth over the long-term. This growth is what produces the high returns that make high tech companies, when they're run well, very good investment prospects.

❷ EARN HIGH REVENUES

The ability to charge a *premium* (a higher price) for the product based on its unique place in the market may create quick, high revenues. Initial production will have to sell out and more need to be made and sold, adding up to growing revenues. If there's any money left over after recouping the costs of production, distribution, sales, and all the expenses incurred in the process, then it can be considered profitable.

❸ REAP HIGH PROFITS

By being the first to bring a product to market, a company avoids some of the pressures of competition. Price pressure, for example, keeps costs down. A competitor might decide to lower profit margins to gain market share. Without that competition, a company is freer to set prices geared to high profits, at least at the start, when customers are more likely to pay a premium for the latest, greatest item in the market.

❹ REINVEST IN R&D

High tech companies with successful new products typically have spent a lot of money on R&D before bringing it to market. With profitable success comes the presumption of a strategy that paid off: All that speculative R&D money was worth it.

To continue as a market leader, however, a company will need to reinvest a significant amount of those profits into more R&D so they can create more new products and start the cycle all over again.

A high tech company, therefore, becomes dependent upon high levels of cash flow, which can continue for a long time if managed well —or dry up quickly, if not managed well.

IS R&D PRODUCTIVE?

Look at:
- Whether a company pours money in one end and has solid revenue coming out the other end;
- How much a company spends on R&D. Usually, spending is efficient because R&D is very competitive inside a company. If the spending isn't producing, you can be sure another department will be lobbying hard for that money;
- The percentage of revenues from products introduced within the last one to three years. If the percentage is over 50% year after year, that success may have a good chance of continuing.

THE FIRST LASER

20th century scientists didn't invent the first light-based weapon (the laser). When the Romans attacked Greek harbors, Archimedes devised one. He took a mirror and shone it on a Roman ship. After a while, the ship caught fire!

PICKING STOCKS

Picking successful investments requires gathering
background information on companies and then
narrowing in on a few that you like.

IDENTIFY OPPORTUNITIES

*Identifying opportunities means looking at the management
teams, products, and markets with which you would like to
associate your money.*

STEP ONE: PICK AREAS OF INTEREST

Picking stocks is a somewhat subjective
endeavor since you probably want to pick
industries and stocks that will hold your
interest over time. Interest makes learning
easier and gives you a better chance of
understanding and staying in touch with the
relevant aspects of the business.

Be sure to think through your decision
rather than rashly buying a stock at any price.
If you understand why you make a decision
and base it on rational thinking, you're less
likely to regret that decision. You will also
then, have a good basis for evaluating and
learning from your assumptions.

▲ PICK A PRODUCT
*If you really like palm pilots, you might begin
by looking at companies that are involved in
making and selling them, making the
components that go into them, and so on.*

FOCUS ON BUSINESS STRATEGIES

Once you've established the businesses that hold your interest and identified some companies involved in those businesses, you might start focusing on the specific strategies of those companies and how well they fit into their particular market. This analysis requires you to move in close and then step back in order to see the big picture, from several angles.

Close up. Consider who's running the company, whether management is experienced, and whether the technology itself is fundamentally sound in concept and practice.

Big picture. Consider the overall market, who's likely to buy the product, whether it appeals to a broad or narrow group of people, whether competitors exist with a similar product, and whether the overall market in that area is strong or weak.

STEP TWO: DECIDE YOUR PRICE

A price worth paying is, of course, a subjective decision, but there are certain things you might look at before determining your price range. For example, are the company's finances solid? If they're losing money, is there a legitimate reason why you could expect that to change?

You can research the overall market and compare stock prices for similar companies at different stages of development. Which one's stock price compares favorably? Do its prospects for near-term success look good? Could the price drop more before going up—if it's going to rise at all? If the price is expected to drop, you might estimate how far down you think it may go, and set that price as your buy point. You may also want to revise that target, depending on how things develop.

STEP THREE: CHECK THE STOCK'S FIT

It's always wise to maintain a good mix of stocks to help offset the risks associated with particular companies, industries, and sectors. How you allocate your assets among the mix depends on your grasp of risk concepts, how to manage risk, your goals as an investor, and your overall areas of interest.

For example, if you're seeking high growth but have a low tolerance for risk, you may want to limit the number of developing companies you own, since they almost always carry a higher risk level than more established ones.

Keep a balance. You may want to strike a balance between sectors and industries. For example, if you see a good prospect among semiconductor stocks but already own a similar company, you would have to decide whether it would be wise to own two similar companies that would likely react similarly to market conditions.

STOCK PICKING GUIDELINES

K nowing how a stock in a particular industry behaves, and what influences those behaviors, is the basis for successful investing. This is especially true for technology stocks, which are prone to cycles based on the time of year and scheduled annual events. Learning to "read the signs" as an insider might, can increase your comfort level, and possibly help to improve your rate of return. Here's a start.

January

Small stocks make it happen
Smaller stocks often lead a technology stock rally into the New Year.

Chase H&Q Conference
This conference in early January puts hundreds of companies and thousands of analysts and portfolio managers in the same arena talking about technology. This tends to cause stocks to move (www.hamquist.com).

February

March

Technology stocks sputter
February and March may be a rough road for technology stocks. Stocks with sharp increases often get sold during these months.

April

Biotech active until April
End-of-year events, such as FDA approvals, the Chase H&Q Healthcare Conference, and high-level churning or consolidation keep biotech stocks active up to April 15.

May

Selling at H&Q
Stocks may rally from the Chase H&Q Technology Conference in January on into mid-May. Professionals tend to buy at the A&E Conference and sell at the H&Q Conference.

June

July

August

Stocks on a roller coaster
Stock-by-stock volatility and modest declines could occur up through Labor Day. People tend to put their money into leisure activities during the summer months instead of investments, creating a lull.

September

Rallies end
Technology stocks may show high volatility from Labor Day through mid-October, which may be the best time to buy. Third quarter reports are due and the AEA conference is around the corner. Wall Street may begin talking more about high tech companies.

Third quarter numbers
Third quarter earnings come out in September. This tends to be an indication of how these companies may fare for the rest of the calender year.

October

Rallies begin
More often than not, the end of October marks the start of a rallying point for technology stocks.

November

AEA Conference
The American Electronics Association (www.aeanet.com) holds its annual convention in November where hundreds of analysts converge to seek out underrated companies and underpriced stock.

December

Race to the holidays
Prior to December 18, investment bankers wait for third quarter figures and then go public with credible deals that were held up during the slow summer months. After December 18 they and institutional buyers are off for the holidays.

Performance enhancers
Portfolio managers, before the December 31 deadline, buy more of what they own, concentrating on smaller stocks in the portfolio. This "window dressing" sometimes boosts prices and hence performance.

FDA approval
Biotech stocks may react on approval announcements made by the Food and Drug Administration before year-end.

STOCKS OR FUNDS?

There are a number of different ways to invest in high tech companies. Here are the two most common ways.

INDIVIDUAL STOCKS

If you want full control over what you buy and sell, setting up an individual portfolio of high tech stocks may be worth the time and effort. You need to continually educate yourself, select a group of companies within those industries, and have the patience to hold on through any ups and downs in price. Investing in individual stocks also involves accepting the risk that some choices may not work out and being willing to learn from mistakes.

Once you decide to buy your own stocks, you can either talk with a broker, use a discount broker, or even go online to trade.

All brokerage firms offer at least some basic education on trading. Many also offer the ability to research and track individual stocks. A full-service broker should provide you with research on any stock you want to follow; that's part of the value of paying for full-service.

Developing a high tech portfolio means following a number of companies in different industries to provide diversity and reduce some of the risk of owning high tech stocks. It also involves knowing when to buy and sell. Last but not least, it means staying up on the news that can affect the companies you own or may own.

BLAME IT ON HIM

The first video game was Pong. It was introduced in 1972 by Noel Bushnell, who later created Atari.

WHICH IS FOR YOU?

The choice you make may depend upon how much time you're willing to commit to tracking your investments, how much risk you're willing to take, and how much control you wish to maintain over your money. Each of these factors are inter-related. For example, if you want more control over your investments, you generally have to commit more time to following them.

MUTUAL FUNDS

If you don't have the time or inclination to handle your own portfolio, you can give some control over to expert portfolio managers. Mutual funds offer a way to own a diverse set of stocks with a significantly smaller time commitment and potentially lower risk. Mutual funds are usually managed by people who have been working in the financial industry for a considerable length of time, know how to balance a portfolio, and often work with a team of analysts who track individual companies for them. This team approach allows the manager to focus on overall strategies that can help capitalize on opportunities while keeping the risk of loss to a minimum.

Mutual funds that focus in high tech stocks will typically commit a minimum of 65% of the assets to high tech stocks, and may own other types of stocks, bonds, and other financial instruments.

Most managers have a particular investment philosophy (also called a *style*). It's important, therefore, to understand the specific approach of a manager before investing. Explanations of investment styles can be found in the prospectus (typically as part of the strategy explanation), are often available online, and can be obtained by calling a fund's toll-free number.

After studying the prospectus, understanding the fund's objective, strategy, style, and risks, you will be in a better position to determine whether or not the fund is compatible with your own objectives. It may also be a good idea to check out the fund's rating. Every mutual fund is rated according to a variety of criteria by independent services such as Lipper's, Barron's, and Morningstar. Ratings are often also available from magazines and online websites.

A fund that fits your needs may be a good option, but be aware that fund managers change, and that past performance is no guarantee of what the fund will do in the future. It may be necessary, therefore, to keep close tabs on any funds you own, or want to own, just as you would watch the stock of an individual company.

CONVERTIBLE BONDS

I f you want a strategy for trying to capture the upside of high tech stocks while lowering the potential risk, consider convertible bonds as an investment.

WHAT IT IS

A convertible bond is a cross between a bond and a stock. It allows you to earn income from interest while also giving you the option to convert it into shares of stock in the same company that issued the bond.

Why do companies issue convertible bonds? One reason is they may believe their stock price is too low and don't want to raise capital by issuing more shares at that price. Another reason might be they believe they can borrow from lenders at lower rates than they could get at a commercial lender (such as a bank).

Convertible bonds are often priced 15% to 25% higher than the stock price. Factoring in interest earned, the payback period, in these cases, is generally two to three years (see the green box).

CALL PROVISION

Be aware that your convertible bond could be *called* before maturity. This means the company has the right to pay you back in full before the due date—the *maturity* date. (It's just like a homeowner paying off a mortgage early.) If you pay another investor more than $1,000 for a bond, then you would lose money if the company calls the bond and repays you only the initial $1,000.

How do you predict this risk? The higher the bond's interest rate is compared to current interest rates, the more likely the bond will be called. Just like a homeowner wanting to refinance, the company might decide to stop paying such a high rate in a lower rate climate.

2 New offerings of convertible bonds are usually not as overpriced as the IPOs of high tech stocks have typically been.

HOW IT WORKS

As an example, you buy a convertible bond and pay $1,000 per bond. The bond pays 7% interest annually, giving you a steady source of income. Each bond you own also gives you the right to convert it into 25 shares of stock of the company issuing the bond.

❶ THE PRICE

If you convert today, each share would cost you $40 ($1,000 divided by 25 shares = $40). The current market price of the stock, however, is only $30, so it would be cheaper for you just to buy the stock than to convert your bond.

❷ THE PREMIUM

The convertible bond you just bought cost $1,000. The cost to own 25 shares in today's market is $750 ($30 X 25 = $750). That means you paid an excess (a *premium*) of 33% ($1,000 is 33% more than $750).

❸ THE PRICE MOVES

Generally speaking, if a convertible bond lets you convert to fewer than 40% of the shares you could buy directly in the market, it won't increase much in value (if at all) even if the stock price rises.

As the stock price rises, however, that percentage will drop. The closer the price climbs toward your conversion price of $40, the more the value of the bond will begin to rise and fall in line with the stock's price movements.

---

3 Buy bonds that are convertible into stocks you'd want to own, not just ones that seem to fit "the numbers."

IS THE BOND WORTH THE PREMIUM?

Consider three factors:

Yield. Whether a bond is worth the premium depends on what might be called the *yield differential*. The yield on the bond in this example is 7% ($70). Assume that, like many high tech stocks, this company's stock pays no dividend so you earn no yield by owning the stock. If, therefore, the stock yield is zero and the bond yield is 7%, the differential is 7%.

Years to earn premium. In the example, you've paid 33% more for the right to convert the bond to 25 shares, but you're earning 7% a year instead of zero from the stock. It would take you slightly more than 3 1/2 years to earn back the 33% premium ($70 X 3.5 years = $245).

Your outlook. You have to decide whether or not 3 1/2 years is too long to wait to break even if the stock price doesn't rise to $40 before then, and how strongly you believe that the stock price will rise above $40 and turn your $40 conversion price into a bargain.

SOME INVESTMENT RISKS

E*very investment involves some type of risk. High tech stocks are no exception. Here are some of the most common risks to your investments.*

VOLATILITY

Volatility refers to the ups and downs of a stock price. If a stock rises and falls frequently, you might consider it to be volatile. If it rises or falls sharply or in large amounts, even if infrequently, you might also consider it to be volatile.

How to assess it. In general, high tech stocks tend to be potentially more volatile than stocks in other sectors of the economy. To see how volatile a stock can be, look at an indicator called a stock's *beta*. The beta compares a stock's volatility to the overall market. A beta of "1" means it tends to be equally volatile to the average stock. The farther the beta goes above "1" the more volatile it tends to be; the farther below "1" the less volatile it tends to be. Ask your broker for a stock's beta.

How important is it? If you think you may soon need to use your money, volatility may be important. For example, a stock price could be rising and falling and you might need to sell during a downswing. If you're a long-term investor (for ten years or more), the short-term swings of a stock price may not be a worry as long as the overall trend is up.

COMPANY RISK

This is the risk that a specific company will falter, either from competition or for internal reasons such as poor management decisions, lack of adequate operating capital, etc.

INDUSTRY RISK

This is the risk that an entire industry will experience a downturn. For example, if the most prominent company in biotechnology has lower-than-expected earnings, investors might flee all of the biotechnology stocks out of fear that other, lesser biotechnology companies will also report poorer earnings.

Another example points out the difference between applied and basic research. Investors might buy biotechnology stocks based on rumors of a breakthrough in cancer research, assuming that the breakthrough will lead to the development of new cancer-related products. If that research fails to materialize, all of the applicable biotechnology stocks might suffer a quick sell-off.

Spreading investments among stocks from a variety of high tech industries can help reduce both industry and company risks.

WILL THE IDEA FLY?

Dr. Samuel Langley was able to fly model airplanes, but on December 8, 1903, his "human carrying flying machine," the aerodrome, plunged into the Potomac River in front of photographers. Reporters made fun of the idea that people could fly. Just nine days later, the Wright brothers proved them wrong.

SECTOR RISK

It's also possible that stocks across the entire high tech sector could suffer losses at the same time. For example, if Congress passes some law with the potential to negatively impact all R&D companies, investors could reduce all of their high tech holdings, no matter what the industry.

Investing in stocks outside the high tech sector can help reduce sector risk by providing diversification. News that might drive some stock prices down, might not affect some of your other holdings.

CURRENCY RISK

Technology is regularly imported to and exported from country to country. The sales of many high tech companies, therefore, can be affected by fluctuations in the currency market. It may be wise to analyze the markets into which a company tends to sell its products. Then follow the exchange rates between those countries and the home country of that company.

THE MORE THINGS CHANGE...

In high tech, as much as in any sector of the economy, change is normal. In fact, change tends to happen rapidly. The sector continually redefines the concept of competition, with new innovations frequently overtaking even recent innovations. Nevertheless, the large established companies in each industry tend to be well-entrenched yet nimble enough to stay at or near the forefront. These companies usually have more money to invest in R&D than smaller competitors. What's more, often times when a new upstart emerges, one of the large companies simply buys it.

OPTIONS FOR PROTECTION

T*here are a number of ways to protect your investments. They involve watching the market and the overall economy and using leverage to offset possible imminent losses to investments you may not be ready to sell.*

OPTIONS AS INSURANCE

Buying *options* is commonly thought of as a risky, speculative strategy. Investors, however, often use options as a type of insurance policy to reduce the risk of a price drop. In essence, the cost of the option becomes their insurance premium, and just like other insurance, they would rather lose the cost of the premium than have to use the insurance.

If you open an options account, your brokerage firm should send you a booklet about trading options. You may also be able to learn about them at a number of different financial websites.

The example in the next column introduces how options work:

> **4** Buying puts can work well if you don't want to sell a stock but are concerned that its price may drop.

HOW THEY WORK

To protect yourself against a drop in a stock's price, you would buy *put* options. There are four main elements of a put, as it's called. For example, you buy a June 40 put at $1.50. Here's what it means, taking one element at a time.

❶ THE PUT

B*uying* one put means you're paying for the right (at your choice—your *option*) to sell 100 shares of a stock.

❷ STRIKE PRICE

The *40* ($40) is the price at which you will have the right to sell your stock, no matter what the actual stock price does.

❸ PRICE

The *$1.50* is the cost of the option—in effect, your insurance premium. Since every option represents 100 shares of stock, the put costs $150.

❹ EXPIRATION

The June means you have until the third Friday in June to decide to sell (to exercise the option) either the put or the stock. If you sell the put, you will earn back whatever it's worth on that date, reducing the cost of your insurance premium.

5 Diversifying your stock portfolio is one of the best ways to protect against a loss in any one stock.

WHEN THE STOCK PRICE CHANGES

If the stock price drops, as you feared, the value of your put will probably increase, offsetting some or all of the stock loss. You now have the option of either selling your put at it's new value, selling your stock at the strike price, or doing nothing. If the stock price rises, the value of the put will probably decrease, offsetting some or all of the gain in the stock. If the stock keeps rising, however, the gain will be more than the cost of your put, which could do no worse than expire worthless. That would mean you paid for insurance you didn't need to use.

◀ **PROTECT YOURSELF**
Options are insurance, just as a helmet and pads can protect you from injury.

OTHER WAYS TO PROTECT INVESTMENTS

Here are other protective strategies to consider.

Picking out-of-favor stocks. It's common for stocks of companies with good future prospects to fall out of favor with investors for a while and drop in price. Professionals call these *undervalued stocks*, meaning they believe the price is below it's true value and will eventually rise to a more reasonable level. When, and to what price, an undervalued stock will rise is anyone's guess, but a stock of a good company that's considered to be at a bargain price may fit one of the first rules of investing: buy low and sell high.

Paying attention to signals. Some investors decide to sell a stock if:

● A company misses two product release deadlines in a row;
● Management is caught lying;
● The CEO resigns with no replacement;
● The CFO quits before an earnings release.

Finding better opportunities. If you have a trading system, you may find opportunities to sell stock at a profit (or a loss) and use the proceeds to purchase other, more attractive, stock.

THE GROWTH FLOW MODEL

Y*ou may be able to spot an opportunity to earn solid returns through a system developed by Michael Murphy, one of the authors of this book. It's called the Growth Flow Model. The name "Growth Flow" comes from its focus on a company's flow of money into R&D, which is the primary way a high tech company invests its money to grow and prosper.*

WHAT IT IS

Growth Flow represents a company's after-tax earnings (called *earnings per share*) plus its expenditures in R&D. In other words, it treats R&D as an addition rather than a deduction, from earnings. Just as some investors look at a stock's price-to-earnings ratio (called the *P/E ratio*), you can also look at its price-to-growth flow ratio.

HOW IT WORKS

1. R&D per share. Start by figuring how much the company reinvested in R&D for the last 12 months:

The total amount spent on R&D for the last four quarters

 The number of shares outstanding

The amount spent on R&D per share

The equation in words. For example, if a company spent $80 million on R&D and has 40 million shares in the market, it spent $2 per share on R&D.

2. Growth flow per share. Now add in the company's earnings per share for the last 12 months:

The amount spent on R&D per share (from #1)

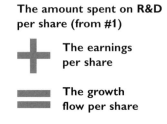 **The earnings per share**

The growth flow per share

The equation in words. For example, if a company spent $2 a share on R&D and has 10¢ of earnings per share, it had $2.10 of growth flow per share.

WHAT'S A FAIR PRICE-TO-GROWTH FLOW RATIO?

- Between 10 and 14 times the growth flow per share (GFPS) is considered fairly valued;
- Below 8 times the GFPS is worth considering;
- Under 5 times should be looked at closely;
- Under 2 times could signal a strong buy;
- Over 16 times is an unlikely candidate;
- Over 20 times is probably not worth considering.

WHY IT'S USEFUL

Since growth flow adds R&D to earnings, a company that looks as though it's doing poorly because of low earnings may instead be a bargain based on the price to growth flow ratio. If the R&D later leads to successful new products and high revenues, investors may reinvest and bid up the price once again.

3. Price-to-growth flow ratio. Now calculate the price-to-growth flow (P/GF) ratio, instead of the traditional price-to-earnings ratio:

The current stock price (what it is today)

The growth flow per share (from #2)

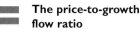

The price-to-growth flow ratio

The equation in words. For example, if the stock is at $15 a share, and the company had $2.10 of growth flow per share, it has a P/GF ratio of about 7:1.

4. The final result. This stock has a price-to-growth flow ratio of about 7:1, or in other words, is selling at about 7 times the growth flow per share (rather than 150 times its earnings per share—$.10 x 150=$15).

Even if reported earnings seem low, or the stock price looks high based on the P/E ratio, the price to growth flow ratio may often identify a worthwhile purchase. Generally the level of R&D spending tends to be stable, rather than dropping with earnings, if a company wants to continue to innovate and compete.

ANALYZING COMPANIES

T*he growth flow model is one of a number of ways you can analyze a company to see how competitive it is and how well it's positioned for the future. Here are a few factors and some thoughts about considering them.*

FOUR IMPORTANT CONSIDERATIONS

When analyzing a company to see whether it's worthy of your investment, you might consider these four key factors.

Sales. When inflation is low, a company with at least 15% annual growth in sales is doing very well. Strong sales may also mean that new products are making past investments in R&D pay off. This is the most important of the four factors, because after all, sales are what business is all about.

Profits. Any company that tries to sell volume on huge discounts could show high sales growth, but if the company also has significant pretax profits, it probably means it has desirable products. *Pretax profits* are sales minus all of the operating expenses before taxes are figured in.

Strong profits also provide the capital to reinvest in R&D and continue competing. Look to see whether a company has at least 15% pretax profits or has some edge over the competition, such as a patent or a large, loyal customer base.

Investment capital. Does the company invest wisely? A company with at least a 15% *return on equity* (net profit divided by shareholders' equity) probably has enough cash to finance its own needs. That can save money, because borrowing money costs more.

Reinvestment decisions. How well does a company reinvest for the future? If it spends at least 7% of its sales revenue (not its profits) on R&D, it's probably focusing on innovation.

THE P/GF RATIO VS THE P/E RATIO

If the price-to-growth flow ratio (P/GF) is smaller than the price-to-earnings ratio (P/E), it may signal a buying opportunity. That's because it's possible that many investors are undervaluing the stock by focusing too much on current earnings and not enough on the R&D that's being spent to generate future innovations that keep the company competitive.

COMPARING R&D TO SALES

If you divide the amount of a company's sales by the amount it spends on R&D, you get the R&D as a percentage of sales. In other words, you're looking at the amount a company takes from sales revenue and gives to its R&D department to spend on innovation.

- If a company allocates a higher percent of sales revenue toward new R&D than it reports as earnings, that's a positive sign.
- The reverse could be a negative sign. For example, if a company's stock price is four times its earnings but it's only spending 3% of sales revenue on R&D, then the company may not be positioning itself for success in the long run.

PLACING R&D IN CONTEXT

Impact on earnings. The more a company spends on R&D the worse its current reported earnings. Under current accounting rules, capital improvements, such as building new factories, can be depreciated over a number of years, which softens the blow to a company's current earnings. R&D, however, is simply an expense which reduces current earnings.

Many high tech companies also don't have the kind of capital improvements that can take advantage of a depreciation tax rule designed for the industrial age.

Traditional company valuations on Wall Street focus heavily on earnings. Consequently, the more a company spends on R&D, the more investors who focus on P/E ratios will tend to avoid it in favor of more profitable companies.

Impact on cash flow. Companies with large R&D budgets are more intent on innovating and staying ahead of the competition than on maintaining high cash flow. That can bode well for the future.

STUDYING P/E RATIOS ▶

One method for viewing performance is the price-to-earnings ratio (P/E). A low P/E in a high tech stock—10 or less—may mean a stock is underpriced. Companies without earnings will not have P/E ratios.

IT'S A FACT

A 1999 survey of 25,500 standard English language words found that 93% were registered as dotcoms.

FUNDAMENTAL AND TECHNICAL ANALYSIS

Most investors take a fundamental approach to their investment strategies. That is, they focus on the qualities that traditionally indicate the future health of a company, its industry, and the overall economy. Others focus entirely on stock charts.

FUNDAMENTAL ANALYSIS

Fundamental analysis is the study of a company's financial strength and basic value. The point is to try to determine what a company might be worth today, and more, what it might be worth in the future. There are many factors analysts evaluate.

Earnings. Analysts may look at items such as net income, earnings per share, the price of a stock versus its company's earnings (P/E ratio), the value of all the shares outstanding (market capitalization), appraisals of a company's value, and prospects for growth (earnings projections).

Equity. It may be informative to see who owns stock in the company. Compare the number of shares outstanding to the amount held by company executives—the *insiders*—to see whether they have as major a stake in the company as do other shareholders.

Financial statements. These look at company revenues, expenses, assets, liabilities, the cash it has to sustain itself, and its cash flow (how and when money is earned and used).

Climate. Fundamental analysts also focus on the impact of the economic climate surrounding a company and its operations.

FINANCIAL DATA

If you're on the Internet, you can access a huge amount of up-to-the-minute—or at least fresh—information to help you monitor the financial status of virtually any publicly traded company. For instance, you can find:

- Annual reports;
- 10-K filings;
- Research and analysis reports;
- Financial e-zines and news services;
- Comparative financial statements on companies.

 6 Some websites analyze the parameters you set. They then return potential investment choices based only on your specific criteria.

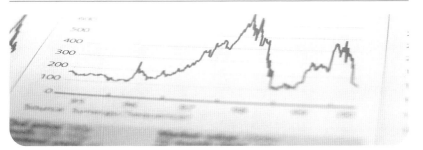

TECHNICAL RESEARCH

While fundamental analysis focuses on a company, technical analysis focuses instead on the stock of the company, treating is as though it has a life of its own. Technical analysis studies a stock's price movements within certain timeframes in order to predict the best times to buy or sell the stock. For example, the focus may be on price highs and lows and the volume of shares traded.

Technical analysis is often called *charting*, because statistics are more easily understood when they can be visualized on a chart or graph.

Technical analysts also use statistics to reveal relationships between a stock's price and other factors. The factors can be any other economic statistic the analyst considers relevant.

The theory in analyzing statistical relationships and movements on a chart is that predictable patterns may develop. If one is spotted, it may be used to help identify the best times to buy or sell a stock.

TECHNICAL DATA

Like fundamental information, possibly all of the statistics you might want to use can be found via the Internet. These include:
- Real-time quotes;
- Financial charts and graphs;
- Trends in stock prices, such as *moving averages* over various specified time periods;
- Indexes that represent collective price movements of groups of stocks with similar characteristics;
- Economic indicators designed to predict future price movements in the market as a whole.

WHERE'S THE PHONE?

In 1889, the first coin-operated phone was installed in a bank in Hartford Connecticut. Soon, pay phones were everywhere. Local calls from a coin-operated phone in the U.S. cost only five cents until 1951. Experts now predict that cell phones will eventually spell the end of pay phones.

INVESTING STRATEGIES

There are probably as many different ways to invest as there are opinions. Everyone is entitled to develop and use what works best for them. Here, however, are two common strategies.

MOMENTUM INVESTING

This strategy involves watching price charts and trying to spot stocks before—or just after—they begin rising in price. Essentially, you try to profit by going along with the momentum of other investors who are beginning to buy a stock in significant quantities. A stock might gain momentum, for example, as a result of news indicating a positive future for the company. It could, however, begin simply because chart watchers noticed something in their monitoring systems that indicated a "buy" signal for the stock.

The key to this strategy is being able to spot a trend rather than a momentary upturn, and in knowing when to sell as the momentum loses energy and comes to a halt.

Trader mentality. In general, momentum investors focus on stocks with histories of significant price swings so they can take advantage of the ups and downs to reap short-term profits. So the strategy may be best for someone with an interest in trading rather than long-term investing.

High tech companies are commonly followed by momentum strategists. That's because the high tech world moves so quickly that investors tend to act quickly in order to take advantage of an important trend. That psychology can cause prices to rise and fall frequently.

**◀ RIDE ▶
THAT WAVE**
Momentum investing is like catching a wave and riding it for as long as the price rise can carry you.

A DISCONNECTED PRESIDENT

During the Civil War, telegraph wires were strung to follow and report battlefield action. There was no telegraph office in the White House, so President Lincoln went across the street to the War Department to get his news.

VALUE INVESTING

Value investing is one of the most common strategies for picking stocks. Its goal is to identify companies that are *undervalued*. In other words, you look for a company that appears to have high earning potential and whose stock, therefore, appears to be at a bargain price.

How it works. Value investing is founded on the premise that stock prices are often out of line with value in the real world. Stock prices fluctuate based on news or information that may not be reliable, and may not, in fact, impact the long-term performance of a company. Therefore, there's often a good basis for making this assumption.

An undervalued stock could be the result of a lack of following by industry analysts. It could also be operating in a market, sector, or industry that's experiencing temporary problems.

Determining whether a stock is undervalued can be as much an art as a science. Some investors use computer models to track stocks and highlight potential prospects based on the model's criteria. Other investors look at the company's fundamentals, such as earnings, revenue, sales, and particularly, the *book value* of the company. Book value is the value of the company according to its accounting books. For example, a company's assets minus its debts equals its net worth. Dividing net worth into the number of shares in the market (shares outstanding), gives you the company's book value per share of stock. If that value is considerably higher than the stock price, it might indicate a buying opportunity.

WHAT'S IN A NAME?

IBM was incorporated in 1911 as the Computer-Tabulating-Recording Co. with a product line that included time clocks, scales, and punch card tabulators. The name was changed in 1924. IBM stands for International Business Machines.

THE INDUSTRIES

The high technology sector is comprised of a number of different industries. This chapter covers one way they can be categorized.

TWO BROAD GROUPINGS

When it comes to evaluating the individual industries, you may want to assess these two groups of companies within each industry using different standards.

ESTABLISHED COMPANIES

These are companies that have been successful over a number of years, regularly produce healthy sales and earnings, and have a track record of remaining competitive in their respective markets.

One way to find established companies is to study several years' worth of annual reports. Reading its financial statements, evaluating its R&D developments and comparing it to other companies within its industry, will give you a good indication of where it stands.

DEVELOPING COMPANIES

Small, developing companies may have little or no sales, very little in the way of reported earnings, and may even be in the red. In the past, companies like these wouldn't even receive a look by investors, but today, with the power of new companies bringing innovations to market seemingly from nowhere, all that has changed.

Developing companies require a different framework for evaluating their profit potential based on what they can reasonably be expected to do and not what they've already accomplished. If a small company has no visible track record, you can look at other factors surrounding it.

Positives factors. You can, for example, see whether a company has any established companies as partners. If the partners are leaders in their fields, you can be reasonably satisfied that those partners have good reasons for the alliance. You can also be relatively sure those influential partners are watching the company closely, similar to how they watch divisions within their own company.

If there are no credible partners, you might also see whether influential people sit on the company's advisory board or whether the company is associated with successful venture capitalists.

Not-so-positive factors. If the company has a terrific PR machine but no strong alliances, it may be a business that's more talk than action. Finally, sometimes even good companies simply don't succeed.

IT'S AN ACRONYM

The letters "MCI" originally stood for Microwave Communications, Inc. No longer used as an acronym, the letters MCI now stand alone.

HOW CAN YOU TELL THE DIFFERENCE?

A combination of size and growth can help you analyze whether a company is participating in the mainstream of an industry. Here are a couple of subjective guidelines:

Developing. A company with around $50-$100 million in annual revenues is still in the transition stage from entrepreneur to established company.

Established. Any company that reaches $500 million in annual revenues is considered established even though it may still have a long way to grow.

▼ **SPRING CHICKEN**
You might consider a developing company as the youngster in the industry, while the established company has already declared its position.

SEMICONDUCTORS

T *he semiconductor is the chip that runs every one of our computers, large and small. It's at the foundation of virtually every advance that occurs in high tech, whether it's the Internet or biotechnology.*

WHAT IT IS

A semiconductor is an extremely thin wafer of silicon. It's layered and etched to form the pathways that electricity will follow to carry information within a computerized system.

◀ **HERE'S WHAT IT LOOKS LIKE**
Virtually every electronic device owes its efficiency to the semiconductor. And the falling prices of all these items is largely due to the constant advances in semiconductors that lead to declining prices for chips.

THE CUSTOMERS

Semiconductor companies serve other companies that make local area networks, computers, broadband networks, wireless communications, storage area networks, and many other businesses. Many other manufacturers, from water softening equipment to engineered plastics, also use semiconductors.

Product designers are the core customers. Only semiconductor companies under consideration during the design phase of products stand a chance of getting in on a new product, since the chip, once selected, is generally inside for the life of the product.

INDUSTRY DRIVERS

Economic cycles drive the industry. In times of low demand, companies don't want to keep inventories of semiconductors they can't immediately use, so they buy only what they need. As demand rises, buyers stock more semiconductors to get ahead of production schedules. When buyers increase orders, manufacturers begin filling partial orders, and step up production. This in turn causes demand to pick up, since buyers fear a shortage may cause them to fall behind. As production increases to meet demand, the cycle can top out, causing prices to dip. No one wants to hold inventory again and the whole cycle repeats itself. In this way, an inventory cycle follows the economic cycle of recessions. Buildup is followed by liquidation, followed by another buildup, and so on.

How Companies Profit

There are three models that seem to work best in the industry.

Owning plants. Building and maintaining semiconductor fabrication facilities is very costly. Not only is the equipment expensive to purchase, it also has to be upgraded fairly regularly to stay competitive. On the other hand, it allows for lower production costs and better schedule control. Initially, low production volumes can't cover operating expenses and depreciation. Once the breakeven point is reached, however, profit margins can soar.

Design without fabrication. Some companies focus on design and marketing without owning a factory. Instead, they contract with several supplier factories, often in foreign countries where costs may be lower. Since they don't control production schedules, costs can rise when demand is high.

Unbeatable patent. A company with a patented product everyone wants can reap high profits. The key is, the design has to offer many different functions and be capable of continually being made faster and cheaper.

Shrinking City Blocks

A quarter-inch square chip of silicon has the processing capacity of the original 1949 ENIAC computer, which occupied a full city block.

Competitive Strategies

There are two winning strategies.

Smaller chips. Making a smaller chip means more chips can be made from the same amount of material. What's more, a smaller chip offers better performance at a lower power because the electron has less distance to cover, so it runs faster and generates less heat. This makes for more reliable performance.

Integration. Integrating more functions onto each chip allows more power to be delivered using fewer chips. This results in a lower cost for the end-product. The lower price helps fuel more demand for the product, producing a cycle of higher profits.

Next Big Change

The next big change in the semiconductor business is the introduction of mixed-signal devices. This involves combining digital and analog signal processing onto a single chip.

In the future, the science of nanotechnology may replace three-dimensional silicon semiconductors with one-dimensional semiconductors such as carbon nanotubes or even DNA.

SEMICONDUCTOR EQUIPMENT

Without the equipment to make seminconductors, there would be no semiconductors—the chips that, more and more, are running everything from cars and appliances to computers.

WHAT IS SEMICONDUCTOR EQUIPMENT?

Semiconductor equipment encompasses a range of machines used to make the silicon wafers and chips that go into many electronic devices. From forming the chip itself and creating the layers, to designing each chip to meet customer specifications, the manufacturing of semiconductors requires a great deal of specialized, precisely designed equipment.

THE CUSTOMERS

Chip manufacturers are the direct customers of equipment manufacturers. Indirectly, however, any manufacturer of a product that contains a chip can have an impact on the health of the semiconductor equipment industry.

WHAT DRIVES THE INDUSTRY?

The semiconductor equipment industry is a cyclical industry. This means that its success follows the rising and falling demand for silicon chips. As consumer demand increases for products that use semiconductor chips, such as cell phones, computers, and digital cameras, the product manufacturers raise their demand for semiconductors. If the manufacturers are at or near capacity production, they have to assess future demand and decide whether or not to boost production. This could mean ordering new equipment or even building new plants.

Since semiconductor equipment is a high-ticket item, it requires a buildup of product demand before reinvesting in new equipment is feasible. That makes expansion a high risk decision, because if demand drops, the new equipment could become an underutilized and needlessly large expense.

How Companies Profit

Since advanced equipment commands a premium price, semiconductor equipment manufacturers can maintain gross profit margins as high as 50%. On average, after expenses, this leaves established manufacturers with a roughly 20% operating profit. Newer companies may have lower margins since they need to invest more in their own equipment.

According to some experts, worldwide semiconductor sales are expected to grow from $150 billion in 1999 to over $300 billion by 2003. This doubling of demand should mean increased growth for the semiconductor equipment industry, as well.

Next Big Change

There are at least three major changes, all based on higher performance and larger production capacity.

Shrinking line widths. The lines being etched into each silicon chip continue to be thinner, allowing for more lines per chip.

Growing wafers. The industry continues to find ways to make larger wafers without sacrificing quality. The larger a wafer, the more chips it can spawn. Larger wafers require new equipment to make them.

New materials. While silicon remains the material of choice, other materials with different properties, such as copper, are being explored seriously.

Competitive Strategies

Introducing new product lines is also critical to success. Continuous improvement in technology, however, is the way semiconductor equipment manufacturers typically compete effectively. Offering the best price for equipment that can build the best chip possible is the only way to attract and keep customers.

Speed to market. It's vital for manufacturers to develop and build new equipment quickly, not only to meet demand but to stay at a pace with the latest technological advances. In addition, customers demand a fast response to their needs. Top quality services by equipment manufacturers include fast production times and installation procedures that are quick and easy.

Customer service. Support in maintaining the equipment for peak performance is also critical, and can be expensive, especially for the smaller companies. An equipment manufacturer may need to restrict its market rather than try to cover every corner of every market.

Lower costs. Most of all, companies who help their customers cut chip fabrication costs should have a competitive place in their industry.

LARGE COMPUTERS

T he large computer industry may be the first in the high tech sector to evolve into something virtually unrecognizable from its former self. Small computing power and the Internet are forcing serious changes.

WHAT IS A LARGE COMPUTER?

The large computer industry consists of mainframe computers (larger than desktop PCs) with the power to run centralized operations for entire corporations. While only a few years ago the industry was focused on building hardware, today business has expanded to include building computers, website servers, networks, and most of all, a full range of strategic solutions associated with information technology.

THE CUSTOMERS

Generally, only very large companies still need the benefits of a large-scale, proprietary mainframe computer. All but the largest applications can run on much smaller computers. Even those customers, however, try to reduce costs and labor by processing as much as possible through small computers.

WHAT DRIVES GROWTH CYCLES?

The industry is experiencing a tricky and expensive change. The need for large, in-house, proprietary computer systems is disappearing. More and more, the Internet is influencing large computer manufacturers. The computing power required to run the Internet—centralized data, networks, desktop computers, software management, and more— is staggering, especially on a worldwide basis.

The industry's cycles are driven by the availability of capital spending by major corporations. For now, however, the vast majority of companies have yet to allocate the money required to retool their businesses to take advantage of the power of the Internet for everything from operations to customer service to instant-feedback marketing,

Eventually, businesses will begin more intense efforts to build around Internet capabilities. At that point, the large computer companies who are prepared with products that are cost-effective, high performance, and reliable, should experience a new wave of growth.

HOW COMPANIES PROFIT

Profit margins have been shrinking ever since the 1980s when companies began exchanging high-end, large computers for industry-standard microprocessors. To compete, large computer companies, such as IBM, took cost cutting measures and lowered prices.

Average gross profit margins are typically around 35%. The most competitive companies spend approximately 7% of that money on R&D. With expensive, one-to-one customer service still a priority, operating profits can be as low as 6%, much lower than during the heydays of the 1970s.

THE NEXT BIG CHANGE

Most of all, the Internet will alter the nature of this business. Proprietary hardware will disappear due to its cost and lack of open compatibility. The computers will support software that's compatible with virtually any other computer. Finally, products developed or optimized for the Internet may also be the products of choice for customers' internal operations (their *intranets*), as well.

COMPETITIVE STRATEGIES

Profit margins are shrinking and the need for proprietary systems is dwindling. Manufacturers are under constant pressure to make their systems compatible with other manufacturers' systems and to increase processing power at lower and lower costs.

It's likely that the large, proprietary computer business will disappear. Companies are hurrying to rethink their large computers as transaction-processing *servers*. The server is the computer that serves as the central warehouse for all data in the system and as the manager of network traffic. The *clients* are almost all desktop computers.

Client/server computing allows businesses to use a desktop computer to instantly access data on the host computer and serve clients' needs more quickly.

As these computers take fuller advantage of the Internet, all data is increasingly being stored so that even cell phones and hand held devices can access them.

SIZE MATTERS

ENIAC, the first electronic computer, was created over 50 years ago. It was 80 feet long, weighed 30 tons, and had 17,000 tubes. Today, a desktop computer can store over a million times more information than an ENIAC, is 50,000 times faster, and has no tubes.

PERSONAL COMPUTERS

The personal computer (PC) has already revolutionized daily life. With more and faster computing power going into smaller and lighter equipment, the revolution is probably far from over.

WHAT IS A PC?

A PC is a self-sufficient device consisting of a central processing unit with input and output devices that can fit on your desktop.

COLLECTORS ITEMS

If you still have one of the first PCs from the 1980s, you may have a treasure. Collectors are beginning to show interest in all kinds of early high tech gadgets. For example, some say that the first Game Boys from Nintendo in 1990 will be collectors' items in just a few years. The original PCs from Apple and IBM may not be far behind.

COMPUTER DEPENDENCY

From the smallest appliance to the biggest mainframe, the average American depends on more than 264 computers a day.

THE CUSTOMERS

Individuals and organizations purchase personal computers, as well as the systems assemblers who buy the components and combine them to end-user specifications. Organizations may buy a few, or a few hundred or more at a time, while an individual will usually buy only one at a time. PC companies that have a broad customer base, mixing individuals and organizations, are going to have somewhat better profit margins, since the sales of larger quantities will require lower advertising expenses.

While some people think the PC market is slowing, the demand is as large as the number of people on the planet. PC sales are growing approximately 15%-18% each year. In the year 2000, over 135 million new PCs were shipped. That was a significant increase over the 112 million PCs sold in 1999.

▶ MOTHERS OF INVENTION
This computer motherboard is a far cry from the first Apple personal computer that was housed in a wooden box.

WHAT DRIVES THE INDUSTRY?

Two areas drive the industry. **Microprocessors.** New microprocessors reduce computing costs and can enable significant advances in software capabilities. Individual users typically increase as a result of cost reductions, while businesses tend to upgrade only when significant advances are made in computing capacity and functionality. Each new version forces down prices of older models until they simply become obsolete.

Operating systems. Corporations will not upgrade without a compelling reason to do so. In short, the benefits must outweigh the costs.

HOW COMPANIES PROFIT

Most companies that sell to end-users rely on their suppliers to carry most of the burden of R&D to help offset their already low profit margins. By spending large amounts on mass marketing and operating expenses, the average operating profits typically run approximately 8% for systems assemblers. Those who build subsystems, however, not only have to skimp on R&D but also have to keep their costs down, typically leaving them with only a 4% average gross profit margin and a smaller net profit margin.

◄ **INFORMATION EVERYWHERE**

Almost every one of today's high tech industries—semiconductor equipment, semiconductors, Internet, communications, software, personal computers, and large mainframe computers—has a hand in allowing the average person instant access to the kind of information once reserved for the privileged few.

COMPETITIVE STRATEGIES

The key strategy for manufacturers is, simply put, to increase computing power. Another important strategy is the so-called "just-in-time" manufacturing, where they can build systems to a customer's individual needs, rather than trying to guess what someone will buy and produce in mass quantities.

Companies selling to assemblers, such as Dell and Gateway, strive for a balance between being the first to introduce improvements and keeping prices low.

NEXT BIG CHANGE

Windows® incorporates a lot of functioning and power. For the first time in the short history of the personal computer, however, it's imaginable that Windows® could be abandoned in favor of new interfaces that capitalize on emerging technologies, such as wireless Internet access on cell phones and other hand held devices.

BIOTECHNOLOGY

B iotechnology may become the most explosive industry the world has ever seen.

WHAT IT IS

Biotechnology is the study and use of every aspect of biology—especially our own—to develop highly targeted products that will promote health, provide preventative strategies, and counteract and even reverse disease.

Despite the limits suggested by its name, the industry actually draws heavily from a combination of biology, chemistry, and physics. Much of the advances in biotechnology are dependent, in fact, on advances made in computer-related industries.

The industry isn't only focused on humans. Advances are also being made in animal treatment and agriculture.

THE CUSTOMERS

Everyone is a customer, even if indirectly, since we all eat, age, and become ill. The most influential, however, are pharmaceutical companies who use breakthroughs to produce new mass market drugs, doctors who perform new techniques using new devices, insurance companies who must approve coverage, and various companies involved in the growth, production, and sale of food and health-related products.

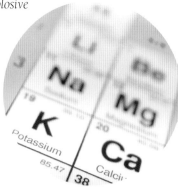

WHAT DRIVES THE INDUSTRY?

Since there are always ill people and animals, and there are always mouths to feed, healthcare and food are non-cyclical businesses. Consequently, biotechnology, which serves those industries, is also a non-cyclical industry.

Growth is driven by R&D, meaning scientific and product-related breakthroughs, both in terms of research and in sales. The industry is at the start of a growth phase that could surpass even the early growth of the Internet. Every new development spurs more new developments, and each success heightens attention to a field.

An aging population with increasing healthcare needs in the major industrialized nations promises to boost growth throughout the industry.

HOW COMPANIES PROFIT

Profitability is largely dependent on how quickly and efficiently a company can operate in a few critical areas.

R&D. Companies need to keep up with the latest basic research and continually apply it to their own R&D.

Approvals. Food and Drug Administration (FDA) approval processes, which can take six years or longer, play a huge role in a company's profitability. While FDA approval requires companies to commit large, speculative investments in time and money, once final approval is given, the product can reap huge profits, especially if it has multiple uses or dominates a market.

Insurers also play a significant role in profitability. Since they must approve a product or treatment for coverage, biotechnology companies collect and analyze economic data during clinical trials to help facilitate insurance acceptance.

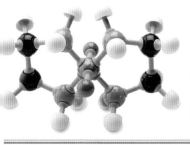

7 Preliminary FDA approval allows clinical trials to begin. Follow the latest news on a company's website or an independent website.

COMPETITIVE STRATEGIES

Shortening the length of time in R&D is of vital importance. Pursuing patents, however, may be the most valuable strategy. Marketing and distribution may not be as crucial as in other high tech industries because so many products are remarkably free of competition. Instead, companies seek alliances with other companies who often license products for sale only within a particular region of the world.

NEXT BIG CHANGE

Biotechnology is only in its infancy and is unpredictable, but many experts believe it will outstrip any growth ever before seen in any industry. At least three new fields hold out great promise to accelerate production of new drugs: gene sequencing, rational-drug design, and combinatorial chemistry.

A PROFITABLE FEW

In 2000, there were approximately 420 biotechnology companies. Only about 40 of them were profitable.

COMMUNICATIONS

Not long ago, data communications and voice communications might have been considered separate industries. Today, with scientific advances, the two can be considered to have merged—with video on the way.

WHAT IT IS

Communications includes any company that contributes to the transferring of data, video, and voice, whether sent by copper wire, fiber optics, or microwaves (wireless). These companies encompass from those who make equipment to those who provide local and long distance services.

THE CUSTOMERS

Virtually any company and anyone worldwide is a customer. With rapid advances in wireless and fiber optics dramatically lowering costs of implementation, huge new markets are emerging in China, India, and many other developing countries.

HOW COMPANIES PROFIT

Average operating profits among industry leaders in telecommunications run around 18%. Data communications typically shows over 20% operating profits.

Hardware companies tend to spend as much as 20% of revenue on R&D but still can reach 20% operating profits.

Since the mid-1990s, fiber optic costs have dropped 99%. This has led to a sooner-than-expected boom in fiber optic communications hardware.

BITS AND COLORS

A voice travelling through copper wire uses the whole width of wire because of a voice's high and low tones. When voice could be converted to digital bits and became all ones and zeros in a stream, you could send many streams down a line at the same time. Copper could carry, for example, 100-200 calls at a time.

INDUSTRY DRIVERS

Communications is growing extremely rapidly, with the explosive acceptance of the Internet, accelerating growth in wireless communications, and the continual networking of the global community. Most of all, however, there's a dramatic convergence occurring between voice, data, and video communications.

There seems to be no cycle. The industry has been growing 30% a year, even through the last recession. No major downturn is expected for roughly the next 10 years. Standards drive growth and are the way understanding is maintained as technology improves. Without an agreed upon standard, information being passed through the world's networks would be meaningless. This is because there would be no effective means of translating the signals into useful information for an end-user.

Now fiber optics is replacing copper wiring, sending voices down paths made of light. Using a prism to divide the white light into thousands of colors, the industry can now send one call down each color of light; more than 500,000 calls through one fiber. Bundle the fibers into one cable and you can transmit huge numbers of calls as bits of data along beams of colored light.

COMPETITIVE STRATEGIES

Cost efficiencies, access to markets, and innovation are the keys to success, staying power, and growth.

NEXT BIG CHANGE

One of the next big steps is replacing electrical switches with fiber optic switches.

As all-optical networks continue to replace copper and electronic networks globally, video data (the largest) will become easier to transmit.

Long distance calls may become so cheap to deliver that it will be free, with phone companies earning revenue from ancillary customer services. It's finally imaginable that virtually every person in the world, in no matter how remote a region, will be able to communicate with virtually anyone else in the world.

◀ **DIGITAL CELLULAR**

Digital technology, turning sounds and images into bits of ones and zeros, is helping to give cell phones clearer reception. Since the data travels through air rather than fiber optic cables, there are no colored lights in the data stream.

INTERNET

The mania in the Internet world has cooled off. Many Internet stock prices dropped as low as 90% off their one-time highs. The industry, however, is still young and growing, providing many investment opportunities.

WHAT IT IS

The Internet is a worldwide network connecting computer and other data communication devices. There are three main areas of business:

- Hardware infrastructure, which is the body of the Internet;
- Software infrastructure, which is the brains of the Internet;
- Content supply, which is the life blood of the Internet.

HEY, LOOK AT ME!

The profile of the average computer virus writer is age 14-24, talented, smart, and driven by a rebellious, adolescent need for attention.

IT'S JUST BUSINESS

At the end of 1999, the highest selling domain name, business.com, went for $7.5 million.

THE CUSTOMERS

The customers essentially fall into two main categories.

Business to consumer. This focuses on providing online services for consumers—everything from retail products to automated services that are designed to make life more convenient and efficient. The business model for delivering products and services to consumers online has had many fits and starts. Only the largest, best known companies may be worth considering since very few show positive earnings, or at least near-term, the potential for positive earnings.

Business to business. This area is approximately five times larger than business-to-consumer. Even so, the companies that follow an advertising or other typical profit model may have trouble generating and sustaining revenue. Furthermore, customers and suppliers are forming their own exchanges and cutting out the middlemen who were the first to capitalize on the Internet's capabilities.

WHAT DRIVES THE INDUSTRY?

The industry is driven by advances in bandwidth that allows bigger files of data to move faster, cost reductions, and increasing options for access to the Internet. While the industry has experienced a major downturn, it's too young yet to tell what areas will cycle with economic upturns and downturns.

HOW COMPANIES PROFIT

So far only the hardware infrastructure segment of the Internet industry is truly profitable. For investors, finding companies that aren't overvalued can still be an issue. For example, the software giants are focusing on integrated packages to dominate the market. If successful, they could push even second tier companies beyond competitiveness. Content supply is crucial but no one has yet defined a workable, sustainable profit model.

COMPETITIVE STRATEGIES

A combination of several, or even all, of the following four strategies will keep an Internet company competitive:

- Being the first to offer a product may help build brand loyalty;
- Securing key partnerships, particularly with the big portals;
- Customizing to consumer preferences, which helps reduce information overload;
- Rapid evolution or staying on top of the competition by looking out for the best new ideas.

NEXT BIG CHANGE

Most likely the business model will continue to shift from advertising in a non-personal manner to more direct, customized marketing. In addition, micro-payments for information content will become more common (as opposed to subscription rates).

◀ DINE ONLINE
La Bastille Internet Cafe in Amsterdam is lined wall to wall with connected computers. It remains to be seen whether Internet cafes will prosper as the world gets wired or whether people will stay online at home.

SOFTWARE

*S*oftware *has traditionally been thought of as individual programs delivered on disks, but it's rapidly becoming the basic infrastructure of both the corporate and home environments.*

WHAT IT IS

Software is an assembly of code sequences that translates someone's computer input into electronic signals for processing and then back into output the person can use. Software enables computers to give people use of applications such as databases, servers, and graphics. In the first generation of personal computers users wrote their own software, but as more consumers took an interest in PCs, a whole industry emerged providing them with packaged software that could serve general purposes such as accounting and word processing. Now it encompasses even more specialized markets such as personnel management, Internet marketing, and online trading.

THE CUSTOMERS

Mainframes and minicomputers still comprise a small portion of the software market, though it's a stable segment. Virtually every company uses software to manage their operations. Individuals are becoming more reliant on software to run a growing amount of their personal lives, so virtually everyone worldwide is a customer.

WHAT DRIVES THE INDUSTRY?

There are two main drivers.

New hardware. The microprocessor dictates new hardware and the range of capabilities the rest of any computer system can handle. Each new microprocessor advance brings with it a growth in software sales, with programs migrating from bigger machines to smaller ones.

New applications. As microprocessors improve, software companies dream up new things to do with all the added power and capability available to them.

Internet. It's now foreseeable that the PC software business could completely evolve from stores, boxes, and disks into programs downloaded through the Internet, especially as line speeds increase. The pay-per-use model may soon become popular, especially as more people access information through palm devices and cell phones. Soon, people may even be paying to store data at a remote site instead of on a hard drive.

How Companies Profit

The software business has been growing 20-25% a year. Some areas are growing slower than others but the areas of growth could keep shifting with each technological advance.

The business is very profitable, with up to 90-95% gross profit margins. This leaves a lot of capital available to the industry for marketing and R&D. Internet delivery could keep those margins high as the costs of distribution and maintenance continue to drop.

Next Big Change

Integrating multi-media with voice input is the next big change to come for software. The voice input application is essential to the functional effectiveness of handheld devices, which don't have room for keyboards. Multi-media, including voice, video and animation will become the standard way to communicate and connect in the near future.

Competitive Strategies

First to market. The goal is to be first in the market with the first software that runs on the new chip, uses the new operating system, or runs on the latest architecture.

Global R&D. Some companies are shifting R&D to locations where parts and labor are cheaper, which also creates around-the-clock efforts. For example, Sun Microsystems now has developers in Russia who work during the U.S. night and send whatever they complete back for continued development in the U.S the next morning.

Integrated packages. As cost savings becomes increasingly vital, many companies will follow the lead of companies such as Oracle and adopt integrated packages that bundle a wide range of software products to manage everything from their websites to their employee retirement plans.

Customer base. The key strategy is to build a base of loyal customers large enough to support continuing improvement. Customers typically stay with a program they know once they learn it because of the time and expense it takes to learn each new program.

Sloppy Floppy

The "Save" icon on Microsoft Word® shows a floppy disk with its shutters on backwards.

COLLECTING INFORMATION

Possibly nowhere else in the investing world is the statement "knowledge is power" more appropriate than in the fast-changing world of high tech stocks.

MEASUREMENTS

Tracking the high tech sector and its individual industries is an important part of an investment strategy. It can help you understand the market before you begin to invest and keep you up to speed with changes that could affect your stock portfolio.

LEADING INDICATORS

Indicators are formulas created to help measure the health of, and spot trends in, the financial world. In general, there are:
- Economic indicators that measure the health of sectors of the economy;
- Market indicators that measure trends in specific markets.

Market indicators, often called *benchmarks*, are commonly used to help measure an investment's performance versus its peers in a specific market, economic sector, or industry.

ECONOMIC INDICATORS

Semiconductors. You can look at monthly orders and shipments of equipment, and at chip sales and orders as indicators of market demand. You can find these figures at www.semichips.org (chip sales) and www.semi.org (equipment).

PC sales. Two companies, IDC and Dataquest, track this market. They often disagree with each other by as much as 3-4% a year. Since the figures vary, the margin of error may be high, so read with caution. Visit www.techweb.com and search for quarterly computer sales.

Internet. The Commerce Department website (www.doc.gov) and the UUNET website (www.uu.net) show numbers on Internet usage and website growth.

Durable goods. Today, orders for durable goods are comprised of mostly high tech equipment.

Newer indicators. These figures aren't widely followed today, but may become more watched in the future because they may indicate changes that affect various high tech industries, such as:
- Medical building starts;
- Knowledge-intensive employment;
- High tech trade balance, rather than the full trade balance.

MARKET INDICATORS

Nasdaq Composite Index. The Nasdaq Composite Index is the benchmark for trends in Nasdaq stocks. It's fairly heavily tilted toward high tech companies because Nasdaq has long been the exchange of choice for high tech companies to list their stocks.

Nasdaq 100 Index. This index focuses only on a select group of 100 companies listed on the Nasdaq. They've been chosen because they provide a good indication of how U.S. high tech companies are faring. The index emphasizes large biotechnology firms, so it may be best used only to track trends in large biotechnology firms.

Nasdaq Biotech Index. This is the biotechnology equivalent of the Nasdaq 100 Index.

Amex Biotech Index. This index is more focused on developing companies than the Nasdaq's biotechnology index.

Street.com Index. This indicates price trends in Internet stocks.

Dow Jones vs Nasdaq. The companies on the Dow are generally considered value companies, while the Nasdaq's are generally considered growth companies. Comparing them may give an indication of the flow of investment money in a particular direction.

INFORMATION RESOURCES

T here are many places to collect information about companies you are interested in, from trade journals to company websites.

PRESS RELEASES

Companies routinely issue press releases on new alliances, product launches, research findings, company restructurings, and any other major development. Almost any change in a company that seems likely to affect public perception, however, will be addressed in press releases that offer the company perspective on what's happening. Whether a release offers hype, damage control, or straight talk is for you to decipher. Press releases are usually worth reading—along with any other reports on the topic—for a balanced view.

OPEN CONFERENCE CALLS

Many companies have begun the practice of holding open conference calls where investors can listen in on discussions among top executives regarding the company's direction and strategies for the future. This allows you to get to know the approach and style of key executives, and get up-to-the-minute details on what the company is doing. Some financial websites alert you to upcoming calls and help you listen in.

INVESTOR RELATIONS

Most companies, especially high tech ones, have a full-time staff member in charge of handling investor queries and preparing information for potential investors. They often compile information packets to mail out, keep websites up-to-date, and handle investor calls, for which companies may keep a separate 800 number. In any case, at the end of their annual report filed with the SEC, most firms list a phone number for such inquiries. A few well-placed questions and you may even get a chance to speak with the CEO, or other top-level executives. High tech firms are generally very eager to find individual investors because they tend to hold stocks longer than professional money managers. Long-term holdings lend stability to prices that might otherwise be volatile; and that looks good for the company.

BERMUDA TRIANGLE UPDATE

Many ships have mysteriously vanished in the Bermuda Triangle. Now all fishing vessels in those waters will be equipped with low-Earth orbit (LEO) satellite systems to continuously track their positions and provide communications by phone, fax, or e-mail.

WHITE PAPERS

A white paper is a scholarly or technical report written to provide information on topics such as research, products, and industry trends. You may find them through a relevant company's website, industry association websites, or various government websites.

Many market research firms release summaries of their study results. You can often find these cited on websites such as www.techweb.com and www.znet.com.

SECURITY AND EXCHANGE COMMISSION FILINGS

The Securities and Exchange Commission (SEC) is the federal regulatory body for the securities industry. It maintains a website with a huge database of information including explanations of each corporate filing. Many of the actual files are also available for download directly from the website.

The database, known as EDGAR (www.sec.gov/edgarhp.htm), is searchable by company name. A listing of the filings available online appears in response to your search request. Filings go back several years, depending upon when the company began filing electronically. Most corporate filings list the names of key executives as well as their investor relations contact phone number.

8 A lot of the news you hear has already been heard by investment professionals and has already been factored into the stock's price.

MORE RESOURCES

T*here are even more places to collect information about companies, industries, science, engineering, and the economy. Some are more reliable than others, but almost all can be useful in their own ways.*

NEWSLETTERS

Newsletters come in a variety of forms, from free versions online (that may be abridged) to fee-based printed versions. There are so many, you may be able to find one on virtually any topic. The credibility of the information depends upon the qualifications of the publisher, editors, and writers involved. They can save you time in following stocks, alert you to important events, or simply point you toward additional sources of information you may find useful.

The longest-running technology newsletter in the world is California Technology Stock Letter. More information is at www.ctsl.com.

WEBSITES

Any high tech company worth investing in has its own website. There, you should find information about the company, and often, links to other relevant websites.

Many companies post their current and previous annual reports, quarterly reports, new product releases, and more. Since high tech investors generally have online access, companies view their websites as a primary tool for reaching their audience.

CHATS AND FORUMS

Live online discussions, known as chats and forums, are an increasingly popular way to discuss stocks, companies, industries, and even personal grievances. Virtually anyone online may participate. Chats and forums can be a useful tool for assessing public opinion of a company and its stock.

In some situations, you may need to download special software. Usually, the website provides a direct link to the download. To participate, select a username and password, then join in.

> **9** Be wary of information from chats. It's been fairly common practice for people to provide misinformation to either boost or drag down a stock's price.

INFORMATION OVERLOAD ▶
Today's problem isn't getting information; it's holding onto only the information you really need.

FOR TECHNICAL INFORMATION ONLINE

Technical charts and graphs view price movements in dozens of different ways. One type is called the *moving average*. It's the average price of the stock as it has changed over a given period of time.

Explore technical analysis. There are many websites to explore that can teach you about technical analysis and charting. Here are a few:

● www.equis.com. Click on the "free" tab for a tutorial and access to charts you can use;

● www.bigcharts.com;

● www.stockcharts.com;

● www.tradingcharts.com.

Get more indepth. Learn about technical analysis, trending charts, indicators, patterns, and also access free charts and graphs at www.clearstation.com. They also have stock screens, news, and quotes.

Technical stock screening. These two sites offer technical stock screening systems which allow you to set parameters and find stocks that match your standards:

● www.alphachart.com/scan.html;

● www.investorama.com/ iqc_scan.html.

Technical and fundamental combined. You can find stock screens that combine both technical and fundamental approaches to research online at www.vectorvest.com.

BULLETIN BOARDS AND MESSAGE BOARDS

Besides chats and forums, you can communicate directly with other investors and with many professionals, through message boards and bulletin boards. There, people can post virtually anything they want to say about anything. For example, anyone can cite a well-known analyst as a source or even quote a fictitious publication or study.

It would be wise to do your own research to follow up on anything you'd tend to believe. See whether the message offers a legitimate link to the analyst or publication quoted. Then go read the text yourself.

One good financial message board is The Silicon Investor board (www.techstocks.com) where the focus is on technology stocks and e-business. It's free. Probably the most popular financial message board is Yahoo! (www.yahoo.com). Anywhere you go, be alert for subtle sales pitches disguised as news.

OTHER RESEARCH

*E*ffective research is vital to investment success. There is so much financial information and tools on the Internet, that it's important to know where and how to efficiently find them.

WHERE TO LOOK

You may want to be attuned to both fundamental and technical factors. Together, they paint a total picture of a company you may be considering as an investment.

You may also want to be in touch with what's happening in the overall market and the economy, and see how your investment choice compares with other companies in the same line of business or sector.

The answers are scattered all over the Internet in reports, analyses, charts, news, and interpretations. It's a broad spectrum, but there are many helpful sites that can take you into the specific areas.

You can find simple to elaborate financial websites giving you free online portfolios, access to fundamental and technical research, stock and broker ratings, and a wealth of links to further financial information. Smart Money (www.smartmoney.com), Money Magazine (www.money.com), and CNBC cable news network (www.cnbc.com) offer a wide variety of research and investment materials and a home page you can customize.

SEARCH ENGINES

Many Internet search engines can direct you to effective research websites and financial articles. Sometimes, however, it's difficult, and annoying, to wade through all their ad hype in search of links to research information. For efficient financial researching, the best engines are often the ones with relatively few ads or blinking banners.

The Lycos Network (www.lycos.com/network) is a popular and well-organized *portal* that includes the Lycos search engine, HotBot engine, and Quote.com, a provider of excellent financial data, quotes and indexes for the U.S. and Canadian markets.

Dogpile (www.dogpile.com) is a clean and easy-to-use metasearch engine with their own directory, along with scans of major and many lesser-known search engines supplying links.

Street Index. This is a compact, no nonsense directory of links to all things traded on the stock exchanges, along with insider news, IPOs, earnings, and index fund links. You can find the website at www.streetindex.com.

MEGASITES AND SUPERSITES

Here are just some of the many sites available to you.

- **Wall Street Research Net**
  (www.wsnr.com). This website distributes a universe of extensive research and information to investors over the Internet. It gives you literally thousands of resources at your fingertips, and claims over 500,000 links to such information as SEC documents, company home pages, annual reports, market analysis, stock quotes, charting graphs, conference calls, global databases, and navigation to all major news websites and financial periodicals. It's a first stop and last resort to accessing anything to do with investment research.

- **InvestorGuide**
  (www.investorguide.com). Type in a stock symbol and click "RESEARCH" to get research reports and charts, with well-organized links to a world of information. Unbiased and comprehensive, it also offers investor education, links to financial publication articles, news, and market analysis.

- **CNET**
  (www.cnet.com). This is a major financial website with news, charts, personal portfolio areas with tracking, quotes, and compilations of brokerages "buy" and "sell" ratings for stocks. You can link to almost anywhere from CNET to access reports and news, and then jump to other supersites.

- **Yahoo!**
  (www.quote.yahoo.com). This website is thought of as a general search engine, but Yahoo! Finance is better described as a huge financial website. There's enough quality research, reports, news, technical charts, analysis, links, and portfolio servicing to keep you anchored for hours. Yahoo! keeps adding services and has become a major financial presence on the Internet.

- **Investor Alley**
  (www.investorsalley.com). For researching overall market trends and seeing how various sectors (groups of companies in the same industry) are faring, this website runs the gamut from breaking news and editorials to research reports, analysis, and trend predictions.

- **The Financial Web**
  (www.financialweb.com). This supersite offers both fundamental and technical research along with services you might not be getting from a deep discount broker. It includes stock and options trackers, real-time quotes, charts, screens, company reports, and an online community.

- **Microsoft Money Central**
  (www.moneycentral.msn.com). This website has columns by insightful analysts as well as portfolio management reports. Check out the Stock Research Wizard and the mutual fund search tool.

MISINFORMATION

*I*ncorrect information takes many forms, from simple misrepresentations *or "fudging," to outright lies and hoaxes. Learning to spot and separate truth from fiction is a skill that's part psychology and part experience.*

ESTABLISHED COMPANIES

An established company that's embroiled in controversy or worried about negative investor reactions to certain events may resort to "fudging" information in an effort to implement damage control. The problem with doing that is it almost always backfires, if not right away, then in the long run. Once the public discovers that a company has fudged information, it tends to be skeptical about the company's truthfulness for a long time.

Overstated revenues. Occasionally, companies try to report earnings before they've actually been achieved. Any time revenues are reported it's wise to put them in context and verify any large jumps through several sources. If you don't have the time or inclination, at least regard revenue reports with some skepticism.

ASSESSING INFORMATION

Here are some tips on assessing the quality and accuracy of information.

- **Credibility.** Look at the credibility of your source. Does this person have the ability to know what s/he is talking about?
- **Corroboration.** Be sure you can corroborate or invalidate the information through other, independent sources;
- **Specificity.** Analyze whether the information you're getting is generalized or specific. Is it rich in verifiable details? Does it all make sense?
- **Skepticism.** You don't necessarily have to disregard information entirely, but it's usually best to regard investment recommendations with some healthy skepticism.

> **10** Don't be shy about calling a company's investor relations department for information. That's what they're there for.

DEVELOPING COMPANIES

One risk of investing in development stage companies is that they may not have much, if any, track record to compare against current earnings reports. This means you have to be a little more vigilant in analyzing the information in its own right.

Market value too high for R&D base. Looking at the market value of the company compared with their spending on R&D can give you an indication whether they are overpriced. Some companies set up separate entities—R&D partnerships—to raise money for their own R&D. Even though that money is actually investment capital, the company counts it as revenue, which makes it look like sales are higher than they really are, and business is better than it really is.

Missing development deadlines. Once a company sets a deadline for developing and launching a product, a variety of things can throw the schedule off track. A company that misses a deadline once should be watched, although it doesn't necessarily indicate a reason to sell your stock. If, however, the revised deadline for the same product is also missed, it could mean that the company is making poor decisions. That might involve a poor choice of suppliers, unrealistic goal-setting, or other issues that may involve poor management skills overall.

ALL COMPANIES

It's fairly common in any company for executives (the "insiders") to sell some of their stock in the company. Many times, it's for personal reasons, but a string of insider sales at one company may signal trouble. Don't use this information alone to make your investment decisions. You could be misinformed of the reasons for the sales.

Many newspapers and websites publish tables showing sales of stock by company executives under a table called "Insider Trading."

SCAMS AND FRAUDS

When being asked to part with your money, let common sense be your guide. Everyone has heard that if it sounds too good to be true it probably is; yet so many people remain willing to suspend their disbelief for the dream of a big winner. Ideas that are really far-fetched aren't likely to succeed, no matter how compelling their presentation.

PONZI SCHEMES

Ponzi schemes are a form of "get-rich-quick" investment scam that can sting unwary investors if they're not careful.

How they work. A ponzi scheme typically involves someone offering you a handsome and quick return on your investment, often with the promise of very low risk. Some sharp crooks, however, put a spin on the usual by luring people to invest while also emphasizing the risk. This gives the crooks an easy excuse when they walk away with the money.

Ponzi artists need many investors. As they collect from some investors, they use the money to repay earlier investors, making it look like a return as promised on the investment. As word of these investors' success gets around, friends and relatives join up, significantly growing the size of the scheme and the pool of money.

Eventually the pool of new investors dries up and the ponzi artist runs out of new money to keep paying off some investors with other investors' money. The ones holding the bag tend to be the investors who signed up toward the end—or the scheme may leave all investors empty-handed.

> **‖** Don't let your "get-rich-quick" investing dreams allow you to trade your common sense for a need to believe—and leave you holding the bag.

12 Wherever you find widely publicized stories of people getting rich quick, you can also find experts at deception.

THE BIG IDEA

If a product idea appeals only to a very small segment of the market, or is simply too difficult to understand—or believe—it may be best to walk away, even if you're afraid of missing out.

Common sense says that for any product to be successful it will have to sell very well, and the narrower the product focus, the less likely high sales will happen.

If a product is difficult to explain or understand, keep in mind that other people like you may not take the time or have the ability to grasp the compelling aspects of the product that would otherwise make them buy it.

CRIME SCREENS

Computer crime quadrupled in three years, according to a 2000 FBI survey. Seventy-five percent of the victims—mostly corporations and government agencies—found that it costs an average of $1 million per intrusion to investigate, repair, and secure their systems once they've been hacked.

SCAMS

Small company scams. *Vaporware* is announcing a product or contract that doesn't exist. This can cause a short-term explosion in the stock, often followed by insider selling and a rapid decline. These are easily detected by the SEC using their market monitoring tools.

Larger company scams. Management desperate to report good quarterly results may ship products on the last day of a quarter to customers who didn't order them. They will be booked as sales and it will take a couple of weeks to straighten out the confusion and put the products back into inventory. The reverse also occurs. Items returned to a company for credit are left sitting on the receiving dock until after the quarter ends, and then taken back in the new quarter.

An example. One company went 14 years without ever reporting a dollar in sales! They originally touted their technology as an early laser printer, then as a digital TV display, then as a communications terminal, and finally as a changeable sign for fast food restaurants. Various Wall Street analysts and investment newsletters recommended the stock from time to time, although no product ever came to fruition. The management and their families sold millions of dollars of insider stock.

Scam protection. Growth flow investing in high quality stocks can't guarantee you will never invest in a scam, but it will help you sidestep the vast majority of them.

WHO PROTECTS YOU?

T*he financial industry is a highly regulated industry. Your best protection is to ask questions and be informed. There are also many rules in place to protect you, and many institutions in place to supervise those rules and assist you when necessary.*

ASK QUESTIONS

Don't be shy about asking—and getting answers to—these questions before investing:

- Is the investment registered? Some types of small companies are not required to register with the SEC, but your state securities regulator and the NASD will have information about any legitimate company issuing stock;
- Is the seller of the investment licensed? Firms and individuals selling investments should be licensed for business in your state. The NASD has this information, as does your state securities regulatory agency;
- Does the investment sound too good to be true? Don't believe in "guaranteed" or "risk-free" returns and claims of astronomical returns over a short period of time.

IS YOUR FINANCIAL REPRESENTATIVE REGISTERED?

Securities professionals associated with an NASD member firm must register with the NASD if they sell or supervise the sale of securities to the public. As part of the registration process, NASD Regulation reviews each applicant's employment and disciplinary histories for any evidence that might disqualify him or her from selling securities to the public. S/he must also:

- Be licensed by his or her respective state securities commissions;
- Have his or her fingerprints submitted to the FBI for a criminal record check;
- Pass a series of comprehensive examinations.

---

13 Some investment firms now have newsletters that track the high tech sector.

PUBLIC RECORDS

Any investor can access the records of securities professionals and members from the NASD Regulation Public Disclosure Program. Information includes criminal convictions and final disciplinary actions taken by any securities regulator. Check them out online at www.nasdr.gov.

FEDERAL GOVERNMENT OVERSIGHT

The framework for securities regulation in the U.S. began with laws passed by Congress in 1940. The primary government agency responsible for administering these laws is the Securities and Exchange Commission (SEC). The SEC was established to maintain the integrity of the securities markets and protect investors. To this end, the SEC requires that public companies disclose meaningful financial and other information to investors, providing a common basis for all to judge if a company's securities are a good investment. The SEC also oversees these other key participants in the securities world:

- Broker-dealers;
- Investment advisors;
- Stock exchanges;
- Mutual funds;
- Public utility holding companies.

INDUSTRY SELF-REGULATION

The SEC delegates regulatory authority to some private member-owned and operated securities industry organizations. The largest of these self-regulatory organizations is the National Association of Securities Dealers (NASD), which has two subsidiaries, NASD Regulation and the Nasdaq Stock Market. For the benefit and protection of investors, the NASD:

- Develops rules and regulations;
- Conducts regulatory reviews of members' business activities;
- Disciplines violators;
- Designs and regulates securities markets and financial services.

INDEX

ACKNOWLEDGMENTS

AUTHORS' ACKNOWLEDGMENTS

The production of this book has called on the skills of many people. Michael wishes to dedicate this book to his mother, Jane A. Murphy, an active technology stock investor who doesn't look a day over 60. We would particularly like to mention our editors at Dorling Kindersley, and our consultant, Nick Clemente. Marc also wishes to dedicate this book to Zachary Robinson for his great patience and support when it was most needed. Special thanks to Teresa Clavasquin for her generous support and assistance.

PUBLISHER'S ACKNOWLEDGMENTS

Dorling Kindersley would like to thank everyone who worked on the Essential Finance series, and the following for their help and participation:

Editorial Stephanie Rubenstein; **Design and Layout** Jill Dupont; **Consultants** Nick Clemente; Skeeter; **Indexer** Rachel Rice; **Proofreader** Stephanie Rubenstein; **Photography** Anthony Nex; **Photographers' Assistants** Howard Linton; **Models** Debra Armstrong, Darby Wilson, Tom Dupont, Bud Lieberman, Ashley Dupont; **Picture Researcher** Mark Dennis; Sam Ruston

AUTHORS' BIOGRAPHIES

Michael Murphy, a Chartered Financial Analyst, has followed technology stocks for over 30 years. He founded and edits the California Technology Stock Letter, a nationally-known investment advisory newsletter specializing in electronics and medical technology stocks. He is the Chief Investment Officer of Murphy Investment Management, a registered investment adviser managing the Murphy New World no-load technology mutual funds. He authored the best-selling business book, *Every Investor's Guide to High-Tech Stocks and Mutual Funds*. He set the world land speed record for Class I/E electric cars on the Bonneville Salt Flats, and works and lives in Half Moon Bay, California.

Marc Robinson is co-founder of Internet-based moneytours.com, a personal finance resource for corporations, universities, credit unions, and other institutions interested in helping their constituents make intelligent decisions about their financial lives. He wrote the original *The Wall Street Journal Guide to Understanding Money and Markets*, created *The Wall Street Journal Guide to Understanding Personal Finance*, co-published a personal finance series with Time Life Books, and wrote a children's book about onomateopia in different languages. In his two decades in the financial services industry, Marc has provided marketing consulting to many top Wall Street firms. He is admitted to practice law in New York State.